W9-ATY-525

SURVIVOR

Jon Krakauer's Adventure on Mt. Everest

Scott P. Werther

HIGH
interest
books

Children's Press®
A Division of Scholastic Inc.
New York / Toronto / London / Auckland / Sydney
Mexico City / New Delhi / Hong Kong
Danbury, Connecticut

Book Design: Laura Stein and Christopher Logan
Contributing Editor: Nel Yomtov

Photo Credits: Cover, pp. 4, 10, 14, 19-20, 23, 31, 34 (bottom)
© Neal Beidleman/Woodfin Camp & Associates;
p. 6 © Tom Kelly/Woodfin Camp & Associates; Maps pp. 9, 12-13
by Christopher Logan; p. 16 © Bettmann/Corbis; pp. 26, 29, 32, 34
(top), 36, 40-41 © Scott Fischer/Woodfin Camp & Associates;
p. 39 © Caroline MacKenzie/Woodfin Camp & Associates

Library of Congress Cataloging-in-Publication Data

Werther, Scott P.
Jon Krakauer's adventure on Mt. Everest / by Scott P. Werther.
    p. cm. — (Survivor)
Includes bibliographical references and index.
Summary: Relates the 1996 experiences of Jon Krakauer, a writer for
Outside magazine, as he joined a group attempting to climb to the
highest point on Earth, the summit of Mt. Everest.
    ISBN 0-516-23902-5 (lib. bdg.) — ISBN 0-516-23488-9 (pbk.)
    1. Mountaineering expeditions—Everest, Mount (China and
Nepal)—Juvenile literature. 2. Mountaineering accidents—Everest,
Mount (China and Nepal)—Juvenile literature. 3. Krakauer, Jon.—
Juvenile literature. [1. Mountaineering—Everest, Mount (China and
Nepal)] I. Title. II. Series.

GV199.44.E85 W47 2002
796.52'2'092—dc21

                                        2001047266

Contents

Introduction

You're standing on the highest point on Earth. Freezing winds rip through your heavy jacket. You've spent the last two months trying to get here, 29,028 feet (8,848 m) above sea level. All you feel is exhaustion and the pain from the bitter cold. Every time you stop moving, you feel frostbite developing on your hands and feet. At this altitude, or height, there is much less oxygen in the air than you are used to. Every breath is a struggle. Your ability to think clearly is much less than it normally is. Yet you've done what few people have ever done—you've climbed to the summit, or top, of Mt. Everest. However, your story doesn't end here. Your adventure in the next few hours will become one of history's most famous tales of human tragedy ... and survival.

Climbers on Everest must wear heavy clothing to protect themselves against the bitter cold.

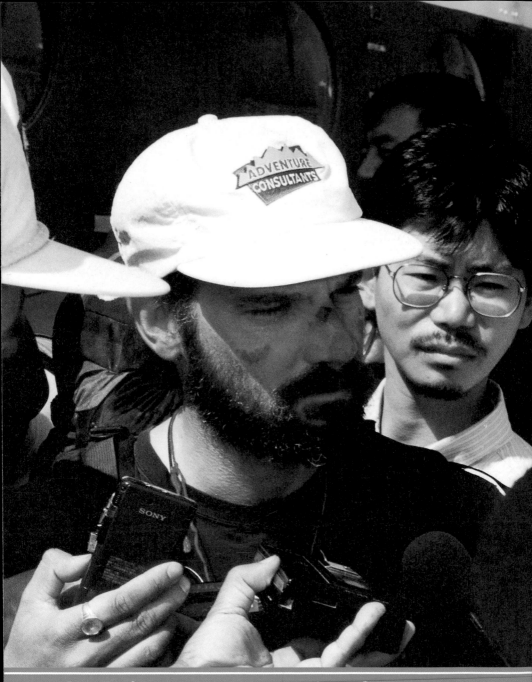

Jon Krakauer answers questions from reporters
after his adventure on Mt. Everest.

One

The Adventure Begins

On March 29, 1996, forty-one-year-old Jon Krakauer, a writer, flew into Kathmandu, Nepal, to begin an assignment. The year before, Krakauer had been asked by *Outside* magazine to write an article about a team of climbers that was going to climb Mt. Everest. Krakauer was an experienced climber himself and the offer interested him. He requested that he be allowed to join the group and attempt the climb with them. *Outside* agreed. For a year, Krakauer prepared for the adventure of his lifetime.

Andy Harris, one of the group's climbing guides, met Krakauer at the Kathmandu airport. The team of twenty-six climbers planned to summit, or reach the top of, Mt. Everest on May 10. Krakauer was excited to be given the opportunity to climb the mountain, yet he was also nervous. He knew that almost one out of every four people who tried to climb Everest never made it down alive. Since 1921, more than 130 people had died trying to summit the mountain.

For many years, only the best climbers in the world attempted to summit Everest. But now, they ran businesses that guided less-experienced clients up the mountain. Some of the people in Krakauer's group had never climbed at very high altitudes before.

Rob Hall, one of the world's top climbers, was the leader of Krakauer's group. He had already summitted Everest several times. Between 1990 and 1995, Hall had led thirty-nine climbers to Everest's peak. Hall's company, Adventure Consultants, was a great success—some of his clients paid as much as $65,000 to be guided up the world's tallest mountain. Krakauer's group was made up of eight clients—seven men and one woman.

To reach the summit of Mt. Everest, Krakauer's group started in Nepal.

China

Tibet

Nepal

▲

MT. EVEREST

India

The Mt. Everest Checklist

Where: Himalayan mountain range, South Asia, on the border of Nepal and China
Height: 29,028 feet (8,848 m)
Age: 30 to 50 million years old
Climate: Average summit temperatures range from -33 degrees Fahrenheit (-36 degrees Celsius) to -2 degrees Fahrenheit (-19 degrees Celsius). Temperatures can drop as low as -76 degrees Fahrenheit (-60 degrees Celsius). Strong, fierce winds and sudden storms are very common.

THE TEAM ASSEMBLES

On March 31, twelve of the twenty-six members of the party flew in a helicopter to Lukla, a town in the Himalayan Mountains. The other members would join the group a short time later. They were at 9,200 feet (2,804 m). From Lukla, they started the long hike to Mt. Everest. That night, the group stayed in a small village called Phakding. They were extremely tired from the hike because of the thin air. They were already beginning to feel the effects of the high altitude—and they still had almost 20,000 feet (6,157 m) to go.

On April 9, Krakauer's group finally reached the three hundred tents that made up Everest

Adventure Consultants Guided Expedition – Spring 1996

There were 26 official members of Krakauer's group. In addition to the 15 listed, there were also 11 Sherpas.

Rob Hall	leader
Mike Groom	guide
Andy Harris	guide
Helen Wilton	Base Camp manager
Dr. Caroline Mackenzie	Base Camp doctor
Doug Hansen	client
Dr. Beck Weathers	client
Yasuko Namba	client
Dr. Stuart Hutchison	client
Frank Fischbeck	client
Lou Kasischke	client
Dr. John Taske	client
Jon Krakauer	client
Susan Allen	trekker
Nancy Hutchison	trekker

Base Camp. The camp was at a height of 17,600 feet (5,364 m). Base Camp was for the many other expeditions from all over the world trying to climb Mt. Everest. These tents housed all of the sleeping, dining, medical, and cooking areas that everyone shared. This would be Krakauer's home for the next four weeks.

Members of Krakauer's group pose for a photo before their summit attempt.

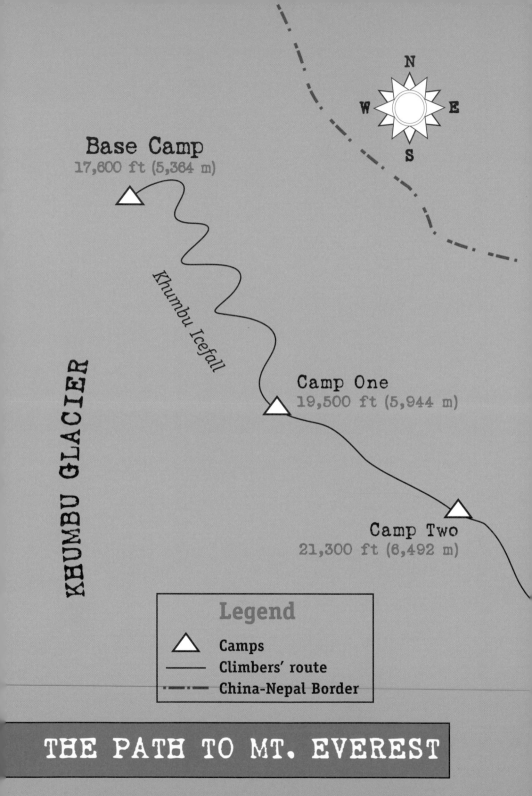

Base Camp
17,600 ft (5,364 m)

Khumbu Icefall

KHUMBU GLACIER

Camp One
19,500 ft (5,944 m)

Camp Two
21,300 ft (6,492 m)

N
W   E
S

Legend

△ Camps
── Climbers' route
·—·—· China-Nepal Border

THE PATH TO MT. EVEREST

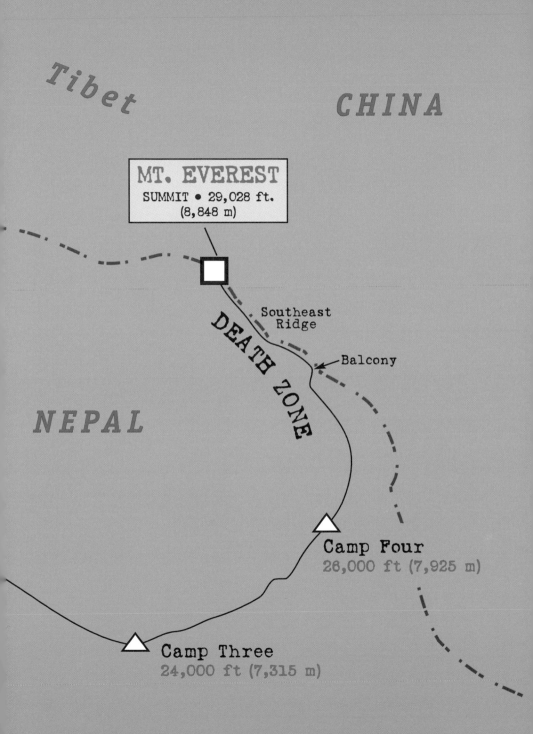

Tibet

CHINA

MT. EVEREST
SUMMIT ● 29,028 ft.
(8,848 m)

Southeast
Ridge

DEATH ZONE

← Balcony

NEPAL

Camp Four
26,000 ft (7,925 m)

Camp Three
24,000 ft (7,315 m)

TWO

The Danger of the Icefall

The first and most dangerous part of the climb to the top of Everest is over the Khumbu Icefall. An icefall is the bottom of a glacier. A glacier is a massive, slow-moving sheet of ice. Even the most experienced climbers take an extreme risk when they cross the icefall. Chunks of the glacier can suddenly break apart and come crashing down the mountain. More climbers have died on the icefall than on any other part of Everest.

NATIVE CLIMBERS

To make the dangerous journey from Base Camp across the icefall, the expedition hired Sherpas to help. Sherpas are Tibetan people who are native to the Himalayan mountain region. They

This climber is using ropes and an aluminum ladder to cross the Khumbu Icefall.

Edmund Hillary (center), was the first man to summit Mt. Everest. Here, he talks with Natar Singh, his climbing assistant (left), and fellow climber E. Cotter (right).

are very strong climbers because their bodies are used to the high altitude.

Sherpas do a lot of the difficult and dangerous work necessary for climbing Everest. They plan out the route and put up rope along it. Climbers attach themselves to this rope with another rope to avoid falling into crevasses, or deep cracks in the ice. Crevasses are often hard to see because they are sometimes covered by snow. Sherpas also place ladders across the crevasses. Climbers use these ladders to climb from one block of ice to another. Because of their dangerous jobs, it is not surprising that more Sherpas have died on Everest than climbers from any other country.

Krakauer's group started across the Khumbu Icefall in the early morning of April 13. Their destination was Camp One, perched on an icy ledge at 19,500 feet (5,944 m). The group moved slowly that day. Some of the more inexperienced climbers had trouble keeping up with the rest of the group. A few of them almost fell off the ladders as they were crossing the crevasses. Once, as Krakauer was crossing a crevasse on a ladder, the ground rumbled beneath him. He tried to stay calm as he heard the roar of an avalanche. Luckily, the falling ice passed 50 yards (45.7 m) away without doing any damage.

BEAUTIFUL, BUT DEADLY

The icefall was as beautiful as it was dangerous. The sunlight shining through the large standing blocks of ice made them appear blue. Walls of rock, with gigantic icicles, were everywhere. Some crevasses were hundreds of feet deep. The tough climb through the icefall revealed the strongest climbers in the group. Doug Hansen, a young postal worker from Seattle, made it easily to Camp One. Krakauer was part of the group that reached Camp One that day, too. A number of climbers failed to make it to Camp One. It was a sign that some of the climbers were not experienced enough to climb Everest. After a rest, Hall had the group return to Base Camp. This was part of Hall's training program for the climbers.

These climbers are carefully crossing a crevasse that is hundreds of feet deep.

Taking a break from the dangerous ascent, a climber stops to enjoy the breathtaking view from Mt. Everest.

Three

The Hardships
of Everest

Breathing becomes more difficult the higher a climber goes. Going up and down from one camp to another was Hall's way of getting the climbers' breathing acclimatized, or used to the high altitudes. They would go back and forth several more times, between camps, before they made a final trip to the summit.

So, on April 17, Hall's group returned to Camp One. The next morning, the group began the difficult 4-mile (6,437 m) hike to Camp Two. This journey would take them to 21,300 feet (6,492 m).

UNPLEASANT DISCOVERIES

As Krakauer approached Camp Two, he saw a large object on the ground wrapped in a blue covering. Light-headedness caused by the high altitude made him confused. It took him a few minutes to realize that the large object was a human body. Later, Hall explained to Krakauer that it was the body of a Sherpa who had died years before. The bodies of people who die on Everest are usually left behind. At such a high altitude, climbers don't have the strength to carry the weight of a body down the mountain.

The group spent a few days at Camp Two. About 120 tents had been set up. They housed climbers from other expeditions, too. Even though the group had a place to rest, conditions were still tough. The altitude continued to make the climbers suffer. Many climbers felt weak and tired. Krakauer got such a bad headache that he couldn't leave his tent for two days. On the third day, he felt well enough to climb a little higher. When he did, he saw the bottom half of another body sticking out of the snow. He could tell from the well-worn boots that the body had been there for at least ten years. Little did he know that tragedy was about to strike again.

An injured climber is being evacuated from Mt. Everest by helicopter.

▶

FIRST LOSS OF LIFE

On April 22, after Hall's group had safely returned to Base Camp to continue the acclimatization process, disaster struck. Ngawang Topche, a Sherpa climbing with a team led by American Scott Fischer, became very ill. Topche was suffering from a dangerous high-altitude sickness. He was carried down the mountain by members of Fischer's team. Topche was then airlifted to a hospital. His condition never improved, however, and he died in mid-June.

PERSISTENCE REWARDED

On April 26, Krakauer's group went from Base Camp to Camp Two in one long day. The group was now ready to make another acclimatization trip—this time to Camp Three. They would be at 24,000 feet (7,315 m). On April 28, the group set out. They soon had to return to Camp Two because of the bitter cold and icy winds. The next day, they tried again. This time, they had better luck. The group made it to Camp Three without trouble.

Sleeping was hard to do because of the difficult breathing at high altitudes. The tired group left the next morning to return to Camp Two. A day later, on May 1, they went back down to Base Camp. The group was terribly exhausted, but the acclimatization process was finally over. Their bodies had become more adjusted to the thin air. The climbers finally found the air at Base Camp tolerable at 17,600 feet (5,364 m). The air at Base Camp that had once been so difficult to breathe now seemed like a relief.

DID YOU KNOW?

*Here are a few of the most famous attempts
to summit Everest:*

- *In 1924, George Leigh Mallory and Andrew Irvine tried
  to reach the summit. Recent evidence shows that they
  never made it. In 1999, the frozen body of Mallory was
  found on Everest by an American climber.*
- *On May 29, 1953, New Zealander Edmund Hillary and
  his Sherpa climbing assistant, Tenzing Norgay, became
  the first people to stand on top of Mt. Everest.*
- *On May 19, 2000, Toshio Yamamoto, a 63-year-old
  Japanese man, became the oldest person
  to summit Everest.*
- *On May 22, 2001, Temba Tsheri Sherpa, 16 years old,
  became the youngest person to summit Everest. In a
  previous attempt in 2000, he lost several fingers
  to frostbite.*
- *On May 25, 2001, American Erik Weihenmayer became
  the first blind climber to summit Everest.*

Four

To the Summit!

After almost a week of much-needed rest, the group left Base Camp for the summit push. At 4:30 A.M. on May 6, Rob Hall led his determined team up the mountain. Krakauer was in a great deal of pain. He described his severe cough "like someone was jabbing a knife beneath his [my] rib." Even ordinary breathing was painful. He had also lost about 20 pounds (9.1 kg), making him more sensitive to the cold air. Doug Hansen, one of the clients whom Krakauer had befriended, was weakened by a throat infection and a bout with frostbite. The group plodded slowly up the mountain and reached Camps One and Two without incident. At this rate, they would be able to begin the final phase of the climb on May 10.

Most of the year, the heavy winds that blast snow off the summit make Everest impossible to climb.

TOUGHING IT OUT

On May 8, the group was climbing to Camp Three. Suddenly, a rock the size of a small television came tumbling down the mountain. It slammed into guide Andy Harris's chest. It knocked him off his feet and left him in a brief state of shock. If Harris had been looking down when the rock hit him, it would have smashed into the top of his head. Was the mountain beginning to turn against the group?

At Camp Three, Krakauer was in charge of chopping ice. The ice would then be melted to make drinking water. Everyone needed to drink at least one gallon of water per day. That's because breathing at high altitudes can cause dehydration. This is a condition that occurs when the body loses too much water. Chopping enough ice to make 12 gallons (45.4 L) of water while at 24,000 feet (7,315 m) is an exhausting job. It took Krakauer three hours.

These canisters contain the oxygen that climbers use when they get close to the summit of Mt. Everest.

BOTTLED OXYGEN AND WEARY CLIMBERS

That night, the guides gave everyone bottled oxygen to use for the rest of the trip. Oxygen was kept in tightly-closed canisters. Climbers breathed the oxygen through masks. The group needed the bottled oxygen because they were about to enter the "Death Zone." With so little oxygen at these heights, climbers run a higher risk of getting deadly illnesses. Brain cells die and even the body's blood thickens.

Unfortunately, Krakauer could not sleep with the uncomfortable oxygen mask over his face. He missed out on much-needed rest that night. By the next morning, Doug Hansen's throat condition had worsened. Hansen had tried unsuccessfully to climb Everest the year before and since then had spent every day thinking about it. More than anything, he wanted to summit Everest this year. Even Scott Fischer, who had been planning to lead his group to the summit on May 10, was tired. He had been greatly weakened by trips up and down the mountain to help his ailing teammates.

MORE BAD NEWS

Krakauer's group made it to Camp Four at 26,000 feet (7,925 m) on the afternoon of May 9. They prepared for the most difficult part of the journey. A powerful storm was blowing, threatening to shred their tents to pieces. As the group got their gear ready for the final push that evening, they received some bad news. A member of a Taiwanese team that was also trying to summit had taken a serious fall earlier that morning. (He later died.) Hall was upset that the Taiwanese team had picked May 10 to go to the top. He knew the dangers of the mountain being crowded with so many climbers.

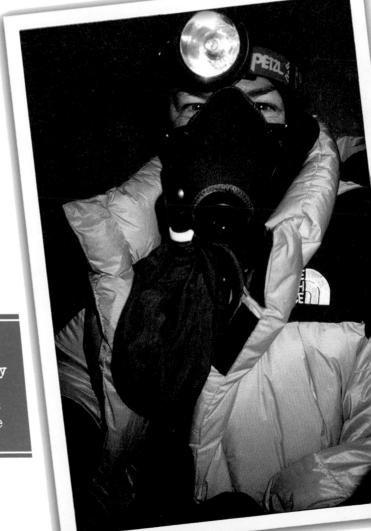

With a head lamp, oxygen mask, and heavy down jacket, this climber is ready to tackle the summit.

RULES FOR THE CLIMB

The winds stopped blowing shortly before midnight and the groups began their ascent. All three teams—Hall's, Fischer's, and the Taiwanese—left for the summit the night of May 10. Hall, who had summitted Everest four times, knew that the climb down from the summit was even more difficult than the climb up. His plan was to have everyone make the return trip to Camp Four during daylight. Even if a climber had not made it to the summit, he or she would have to turn back by 1:00 or 2:00 P.M. This would allow the team to make the best use of the daylight. He also wanted them to be back at Camp Four by 5:00 P.M.—before their supplies of bottled oxygen would run out. It was now a race against time.

Doug Hansen watches a long line of climbers as they make their way toward the summit.

A full moon casts an eerie glow over the summit of Mt. Everest (top).

UNABLE TO CONTINUE

The moon rose over a nearby mountain as thirty-four people set out in a line to summit Everest. One member of Krakauer's group dropped out and descended to the tents a few hours after starting. Doug Hansen also stepped out of the line of climbers. After a brief conversation with Hall, Hansen decided to continue. No one knows what was said, but it was a mistake that would cost Hansen his life.

By sunrise, a few more clients had dropped out. After months of preparation, it was a difficult decision to turn back, but a very wise one. Meanwhile, the long line of climbers from the three expeditions began to slow down in some of the more difficult spots. Precious time was being wasted.

REALIZING HIS DREAM

Passing the slower climbers, Krakauer kept climbing. After completing the last difficult

The Hillary Step is one of the most difficult
sections of the climb.

section, he was only a few feet away from the summit. Exhausted, he saw that there was no place higher to climb. Krakauer had finally reached the top of the world. It was just after 1:00 P.M. He had kept to Hall's schedule. He snapped a few pictures and took in the magnificent view.

But Krakauer knew what was ahead. His climb down to the safety of Camp Four would be even tougher.

THE CLIMB DOWN

As Krakauer made his way down, he passed a number of climbers still on their way up. Behind them, dark storm clouds were blowing in. It was past 2:00 P.M. now. Krakauer was confused because he thought everyone was to turn around by 2:00 P.M.—no matter where they were. Krakauer passed Andy Harris, who was exhausted but seemed to be doing well. He also passed Rob Hall, Scott Fischer, and Doug Hansen. It was the last time he would ever see the four men again.

BACK AT CAMP

At about 7:00 P.M., Krakauer made it back to Camp Four. He collapsed in his tent, not knowing that there were nineteen men and women trapped on the mountain—fighting for their lives. The storm moved in quickly. It made the already difficult climb a deadly one. The whipping wind had picked up and the temperatures became even colder. The blowing snow made seeing almost impossible. Climbers became separated from one another. Everything was going wrong. Why hadn't the climbers turned back?

DISASTER

As the night dragged on, Hall became too weak to continue his climb. The frigid storm had trapped him high on the mountain. He survived the night but by the next day he was dead. Harris, who had tried to help Hall, got lost in the storm and died, too. Hansen also froze to death. Fischer made sure his entire team got down safely, but he was too weak to continue down himself. Like Hall, he survived the night but died the next day. On the following day, May 11, a member of Krakauer's group found the remaining survivors and led them to Camp Four. In total, eight people lost their lives on Everest. From Krakauer's group the victims were Rob Hall, Doug Hansen, Andy Harris, and Yasuko Namba, a female client. Scott Fischer and three Sherpa climbers also perished. A thrilling six-week adventure had ended in tragedy in one night.

EPILOGUE

The next morning, Krakauer and the surviving members of his group sadly began the journey down the mountain. They were shocked by the deaths of their friends. What could have been a joyful

Rob Hall was a talented climber and experienced leader who lost his life on Everest.

success had turned into a personal nightmare for everyone. There were many reasons for the tragedy on Everest. Many climbers were inexperienced and did not realize the seriousness of the storm. Perhaps their perception of reality was clouded by the lack of oxygen and their strong desire to attain a lifelong dream. No one will ever know for sure.

For the survivors who continue to relive the Everest tragedy, surviving the climb was a personal triumph over death. By pushing themselves beyond the limits of their physical and emotional capabilities, they escaped the fate of their companions. None of them will ever forget their adventure on the top of the world and their struggle to survive.

Scott Fischer died on Mt. Everest after helping his team to safety.

acclimatize to get used to a new temperature, altitude, climate, environment, or situation

altitude the height of something above sea level

ascent the act or process of climbing upward

attain to gain or achieve by effort

avalanche a large mass of snow, ice, and rock that slides down a mountain

client a person who pays for someone's services

crevasse a deep crack in a large body of ice

dehydration when the body loses too much water

expedition a trip made by a group of people with a specific purpose

frostbite an injury to a part of the body caused by exposure to freezing temperatures

NEW WORDS

glacier a large mass of ice moving very slowly down a mountain or along a valley

icefall blocks of ice that are part of a glacier

route a pathway or course for traveling from one place to another

summit (noun) the highest point or part

summit (verb) to reach the top of a mountain

FOR FURTHER READING

Krakauer, Jon. *Into Thin Air.* New York: Anchor Books, 1999.

Jenkins, Steve. *The Top of the World: Climbing Mount Everest.* Boston: Houghton Mifflin, 1999.

Pfetzer, Mark and Jack Galvin. *Within Reach: My Everest Story.* New York: Penguin Putnam, 1998.

Platt, Richard. *Everest: Reaching the World's Highest Peak.* New York: DK Publishing, 2000.

Stevens, Rebecca. *Everest.* New York: DK Publishing, 2001.

RESOURCES

NOVA Online: Lost on Everest

www.pbs.org/wgbh/nova/everest

This site about climbing Everest includes information on the 1996 tragedy and a history of Everest climbers.

Outside Magazine

http://www.outsidemag.com/magazine/0996/9609feev.html

This is the article that Jon Krakauer wrote shortly after returning to the United States.

Everest News

www.everestnews.com

This site has up-to-date news on past and present Everest expeditions.

Mount Everest.com

www.mteverest.com

This Web site provides links to other sites for more information about Mt. Everest.

INDEX

INDEX

Scott Werther is an editor and freelance writer from Monkton, MD. He recommends that all readers spend some time in the outdoors.